ICan't Afford the Internet Anymore:

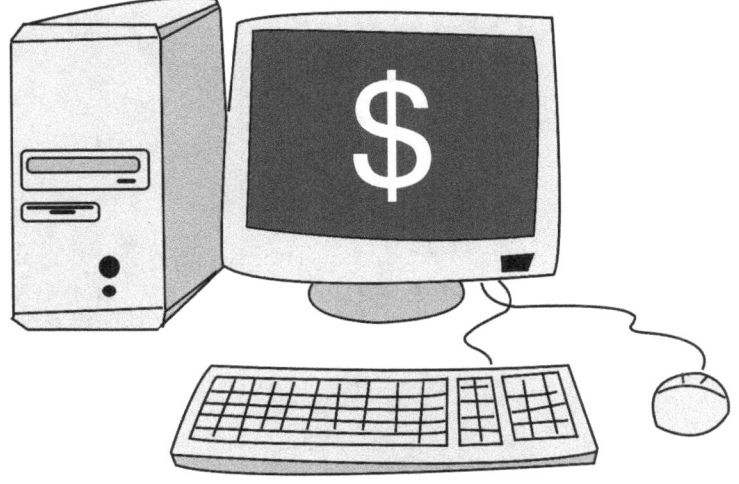

A Net Neutrality Coloring Coping Book

Creators:

Timothy Carambat

&

Madison Hannan

DEDICATION

To the Internet, as we all knew it.

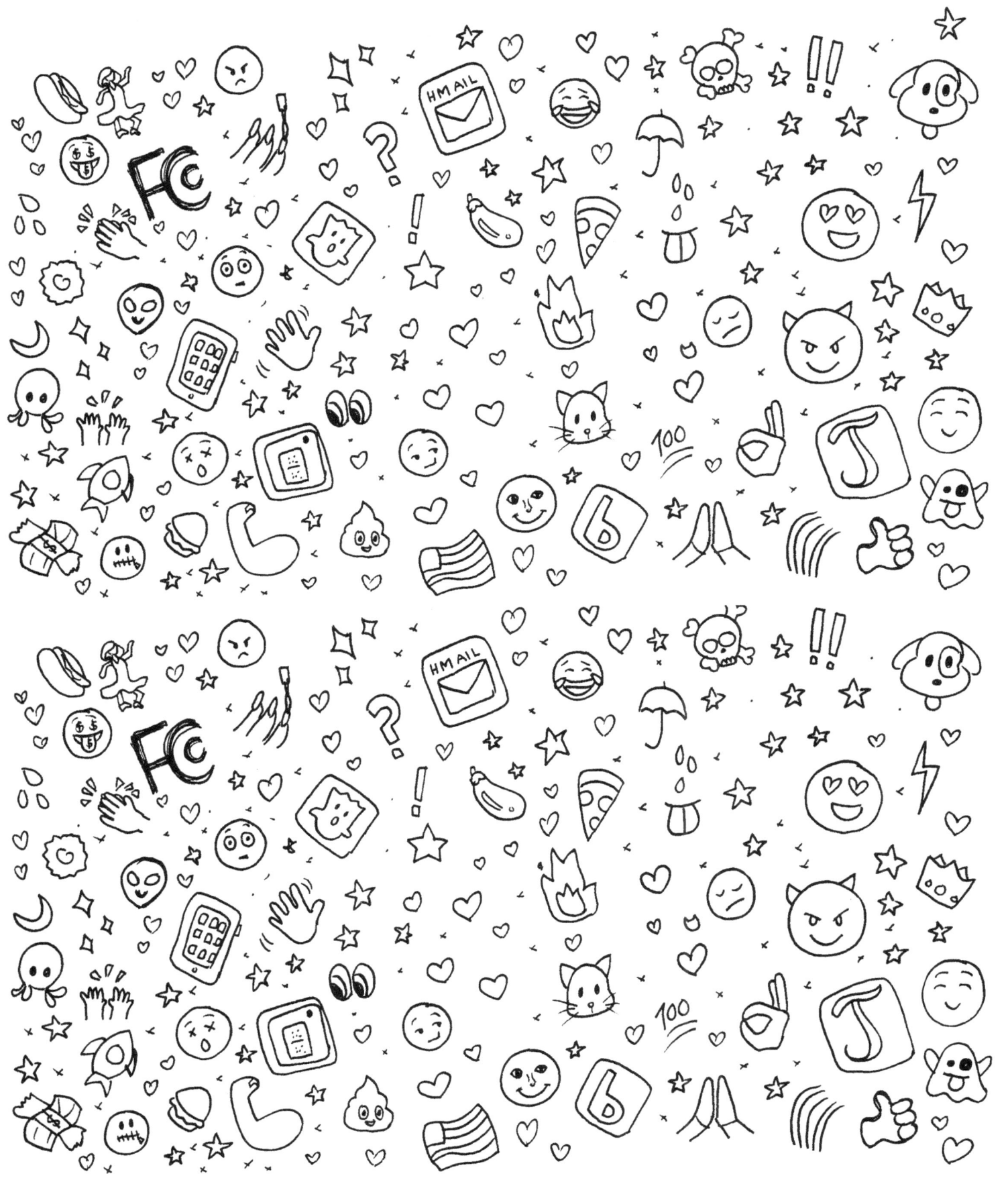

>contents. txt

Net Neu-What?

For those who are picking this up and aren't sure what this is even about, it's a coloring book that shows what the internet was and might become since the repeal of Net Neutrality.

Net Neutrality: the principle that Internet service providers should enable access to <u>all</u> content and applications regardless of the source, and without <u>favoring</u> or <u>blocking</u> particular products or websites from its customers.

Using this book can give you a small taste of what the post-net-neutrality internet might be. Any kind of references to existing platforms or services is purely coincidental.

Flip to the end for references on what you can do to restore net neutrality should you feel so inclined after seeing what your internet service and experience may become.

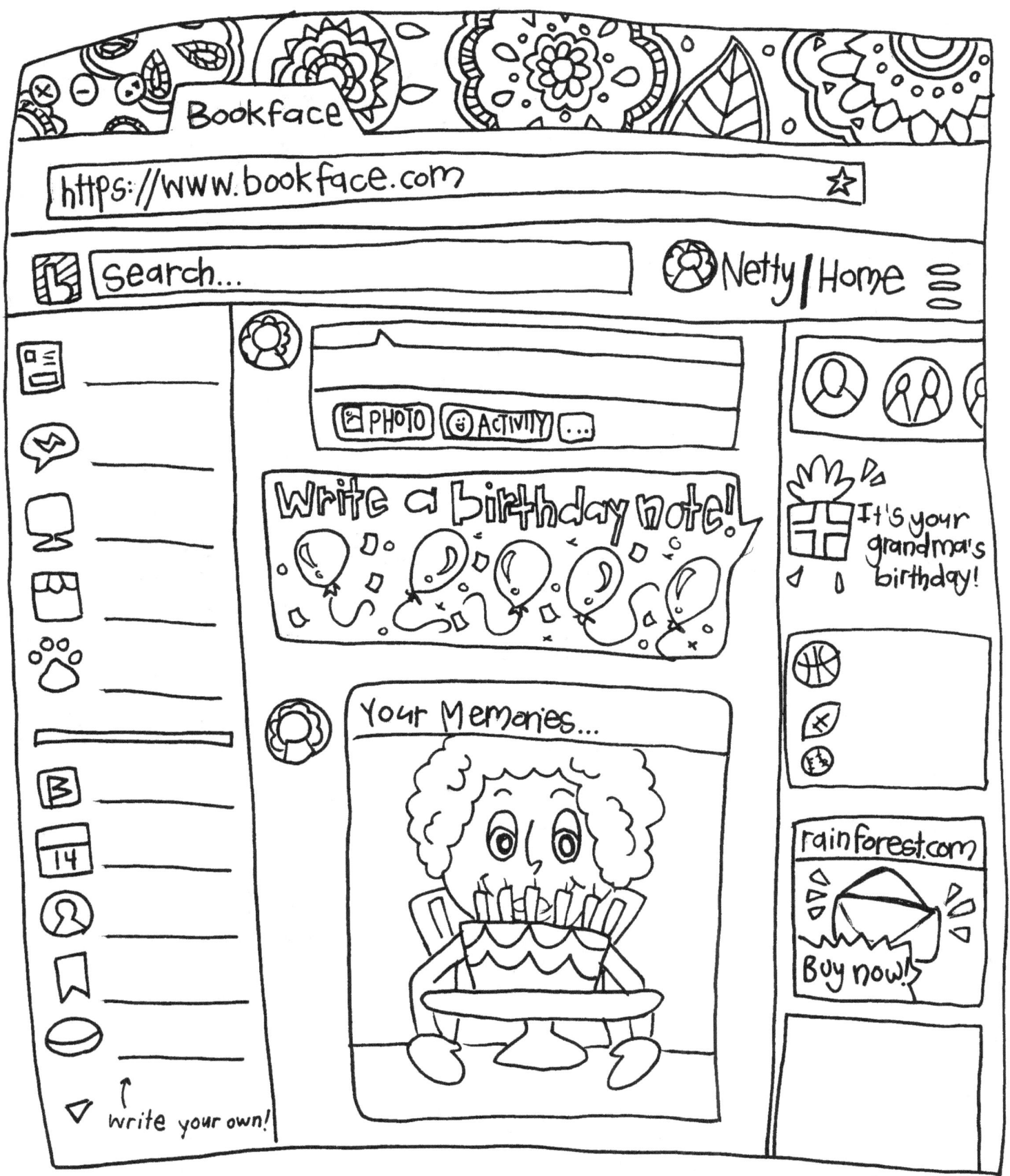

Happy Birthday Grandma!

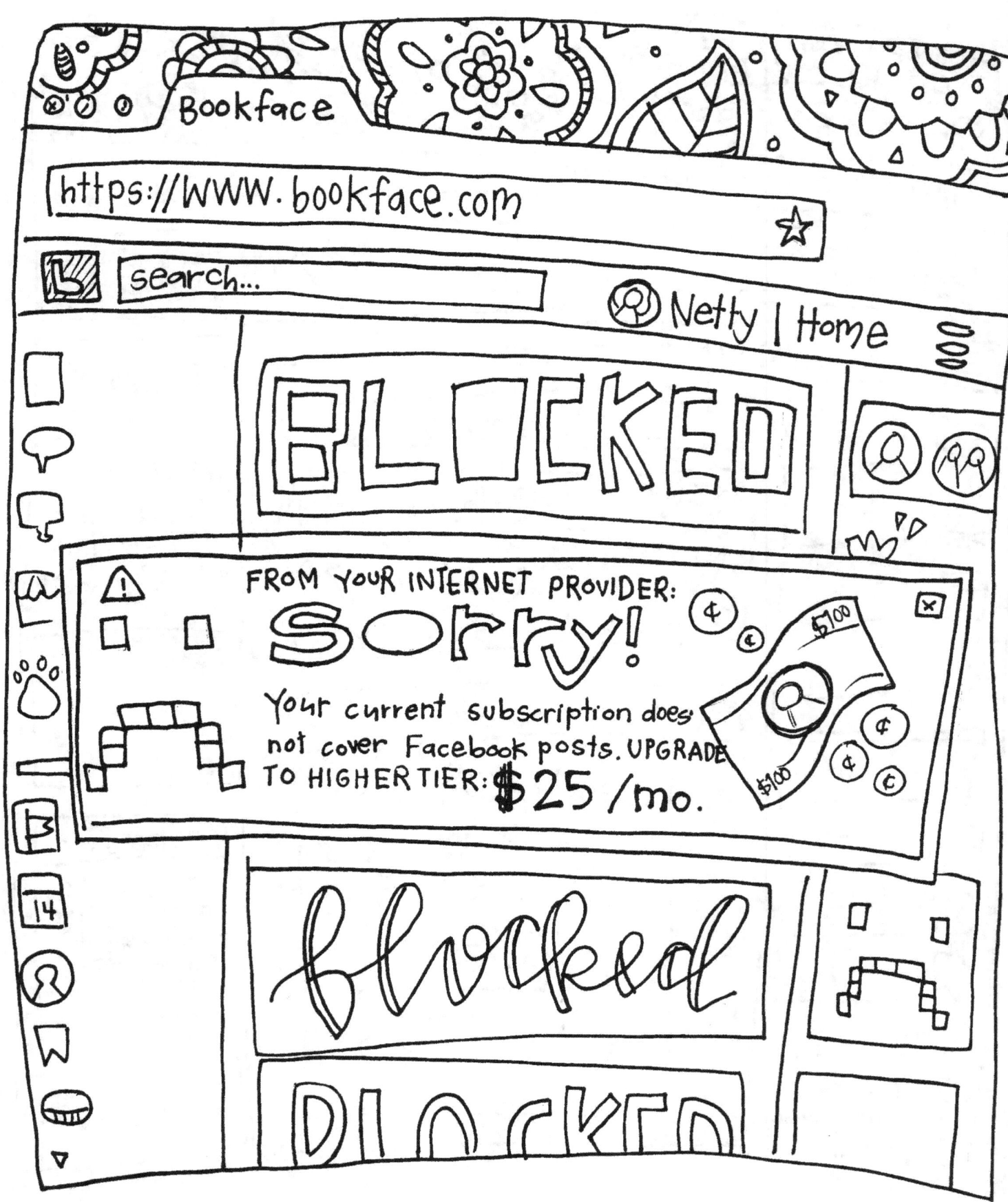

...Maybe you could mail her a card or something?

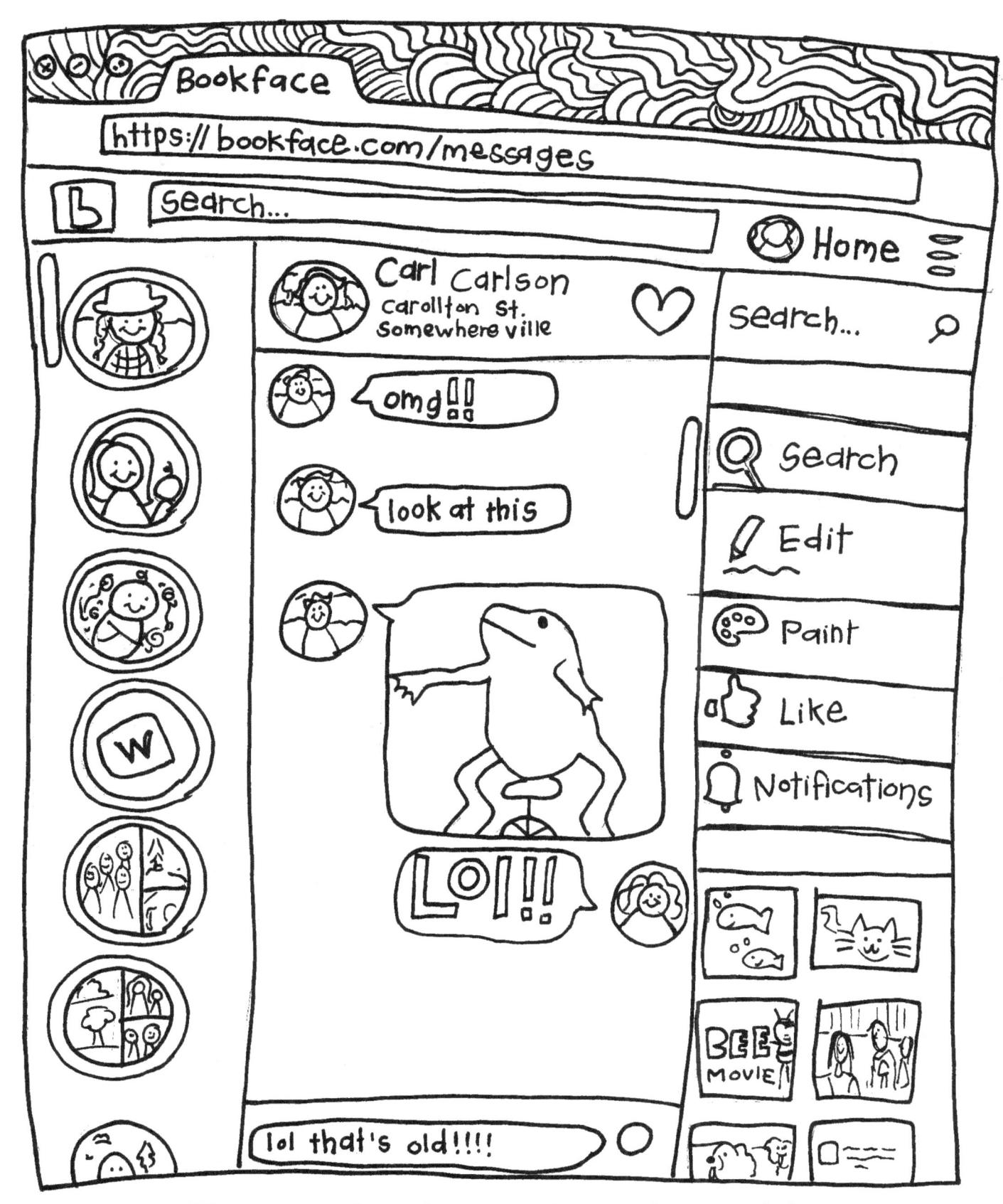

Tag friends in the
newest memes

3

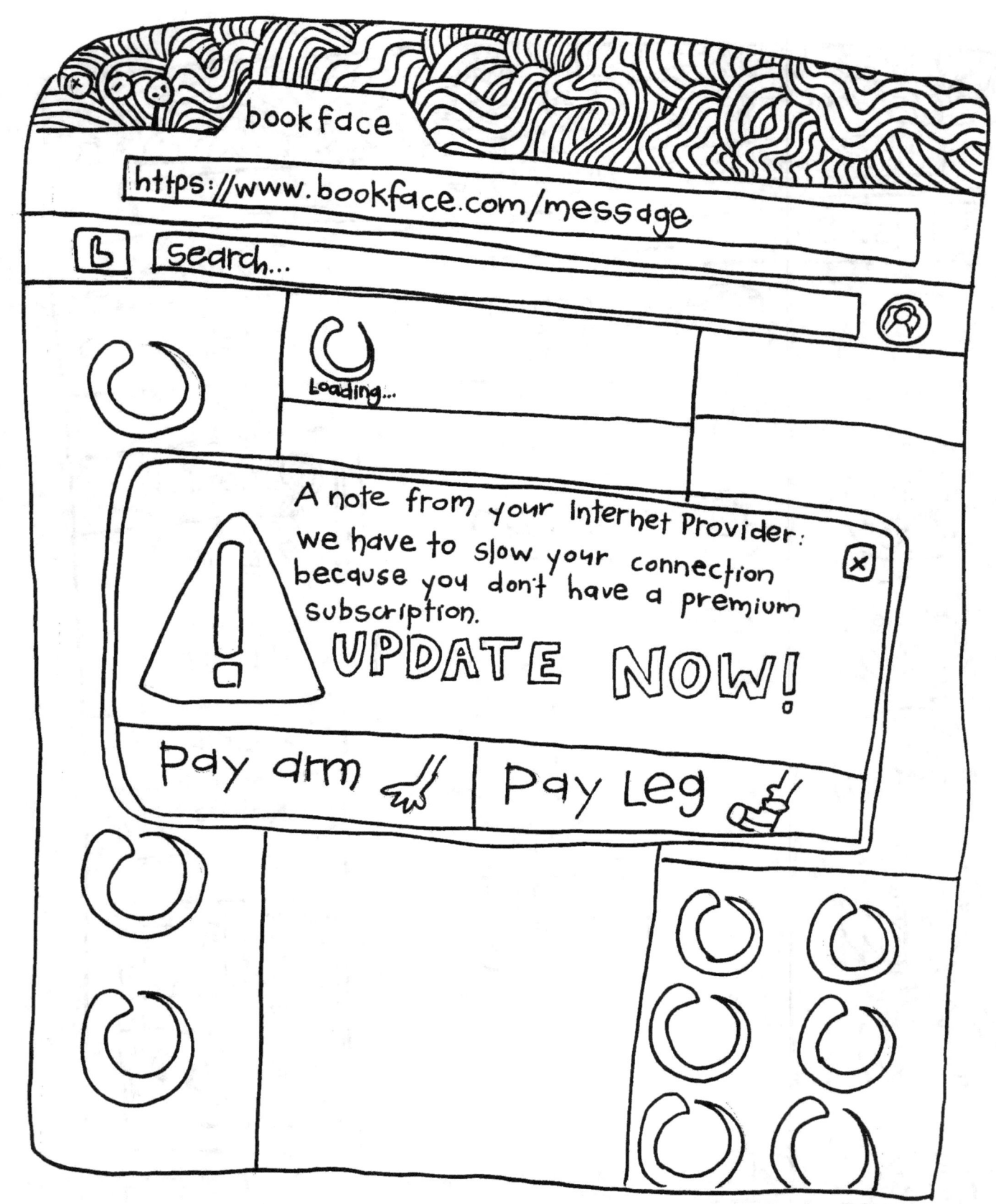

Oh...maybe you could just tell them about it later...

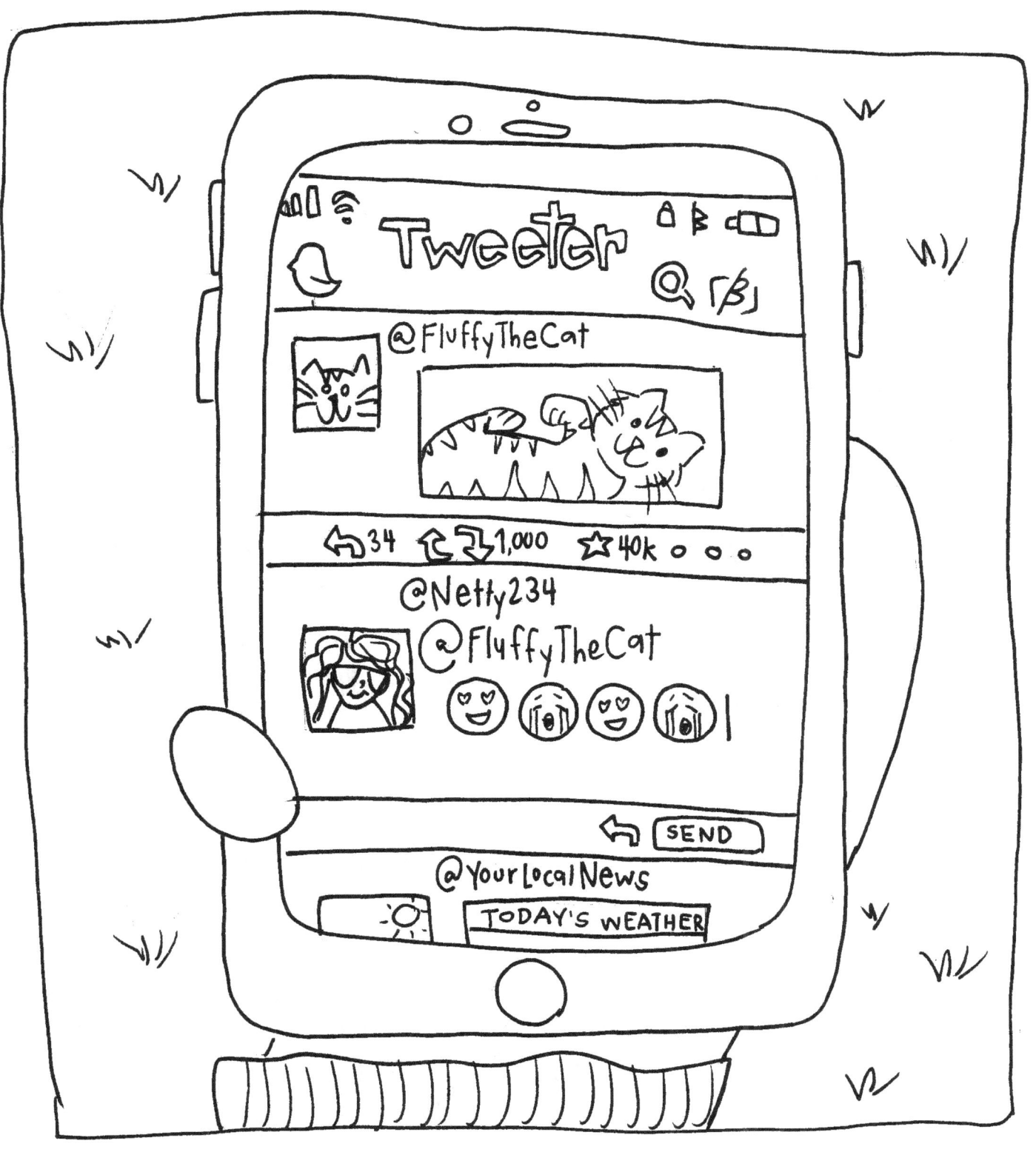

Keep up with all the
celebrities, memes and news
as it happens.

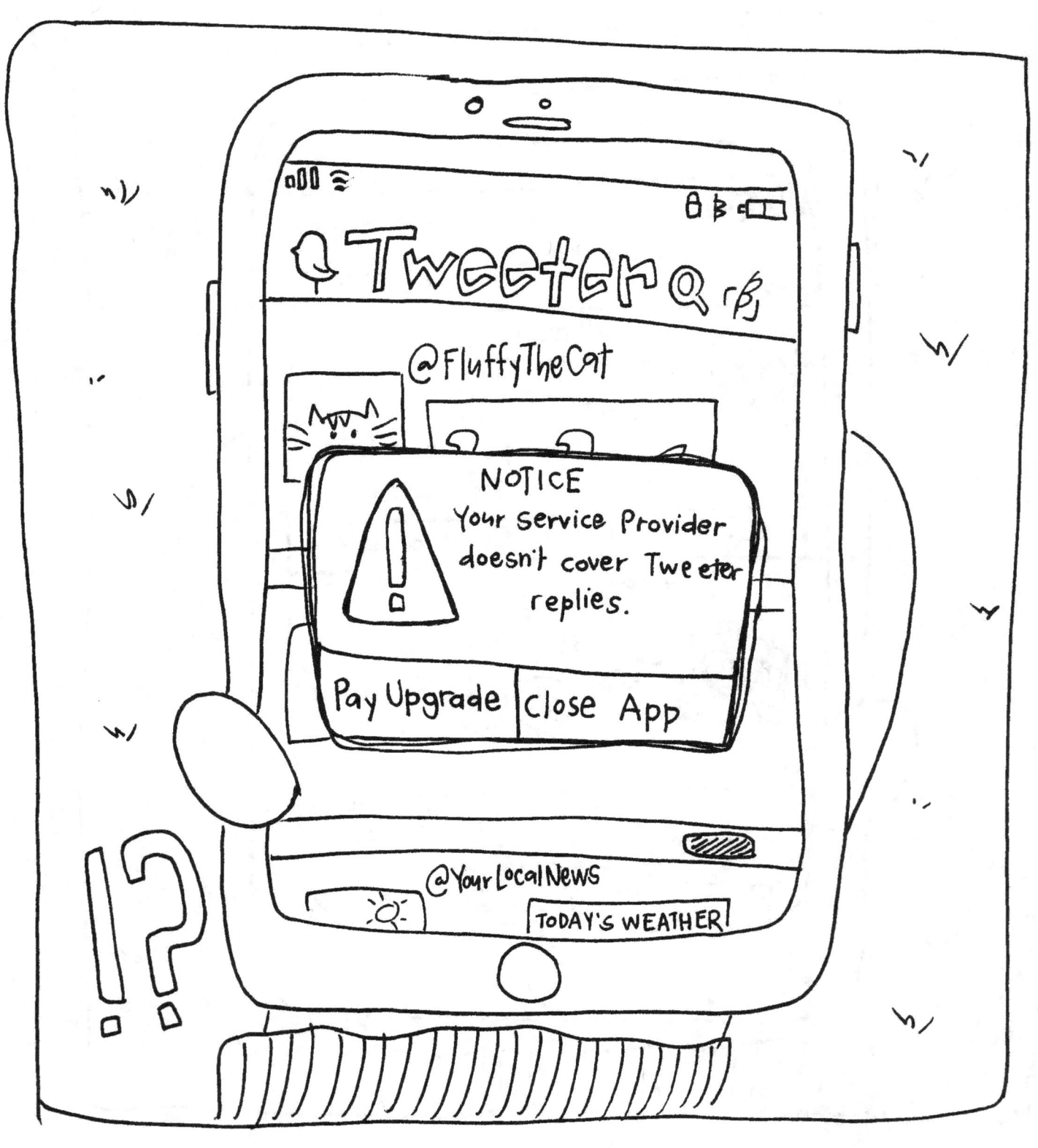

Do they even publish memes
in newspapers?

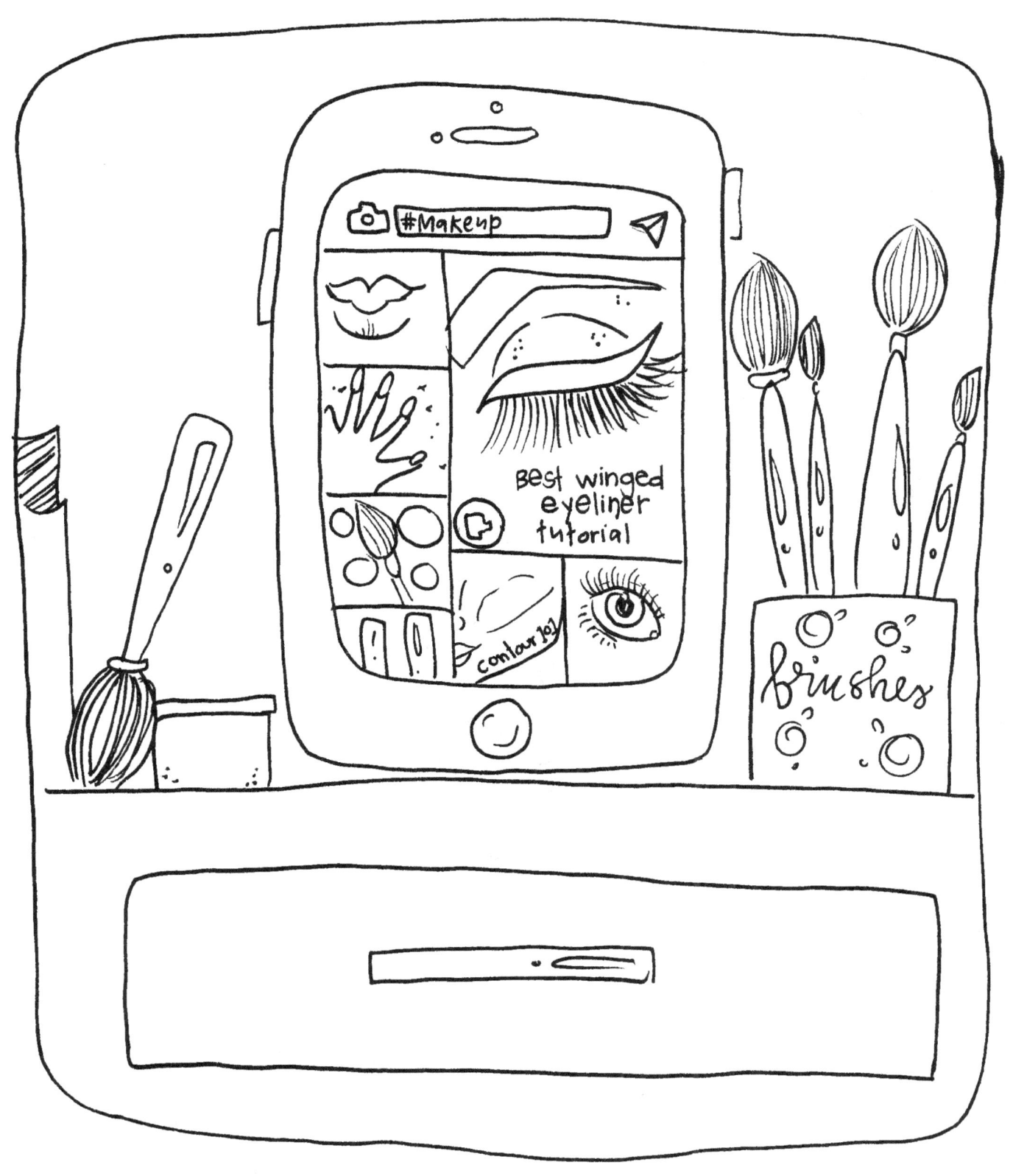

Watch 55 makeup tutorials to
get the wing just right. 7

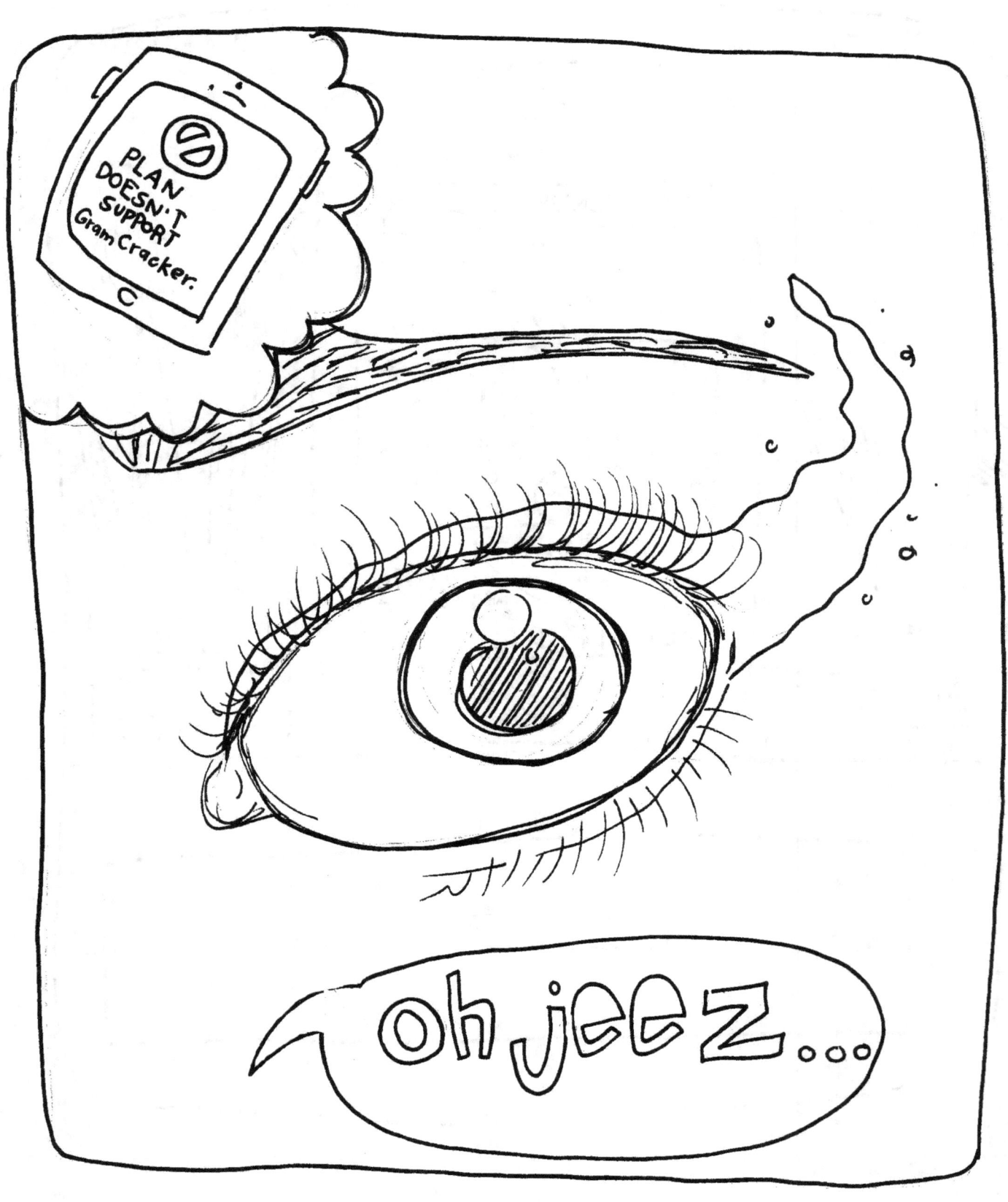

...Guess you're gonna have to figure out that one.

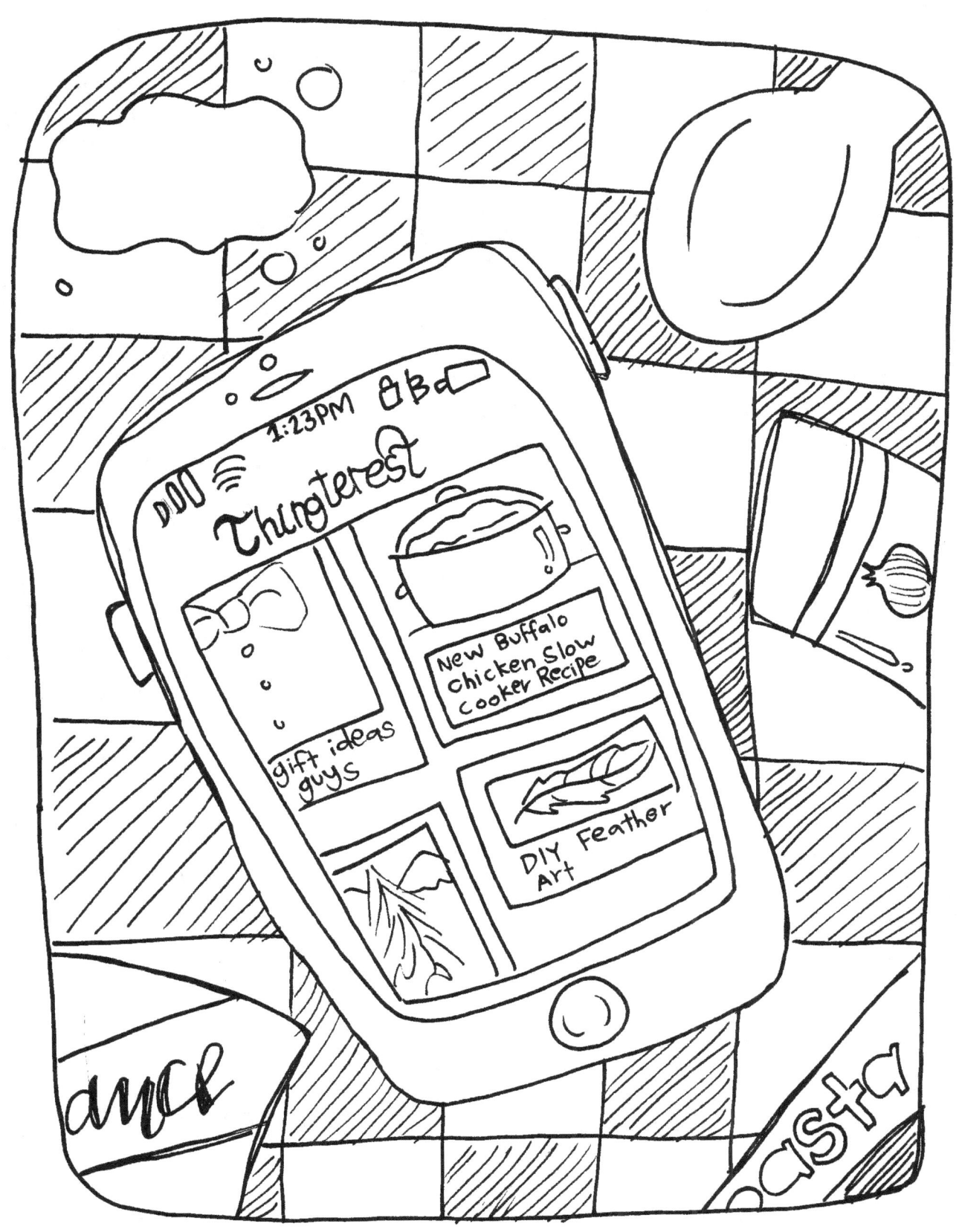

Share recipes, gift ideas, and
all the cool new stuff. 9

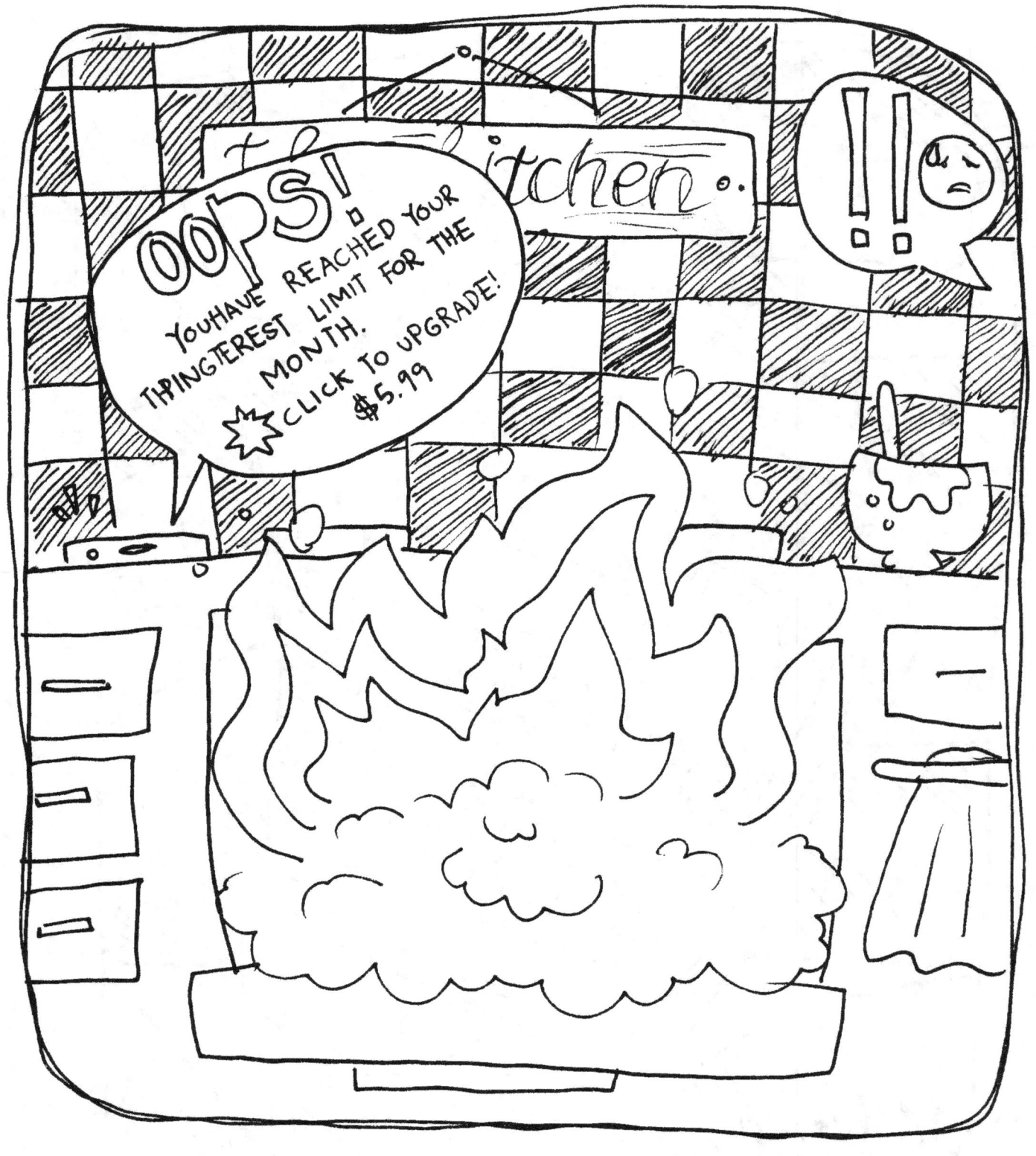

You could just collect the
recipes on the back of the
box...it's the same thing.

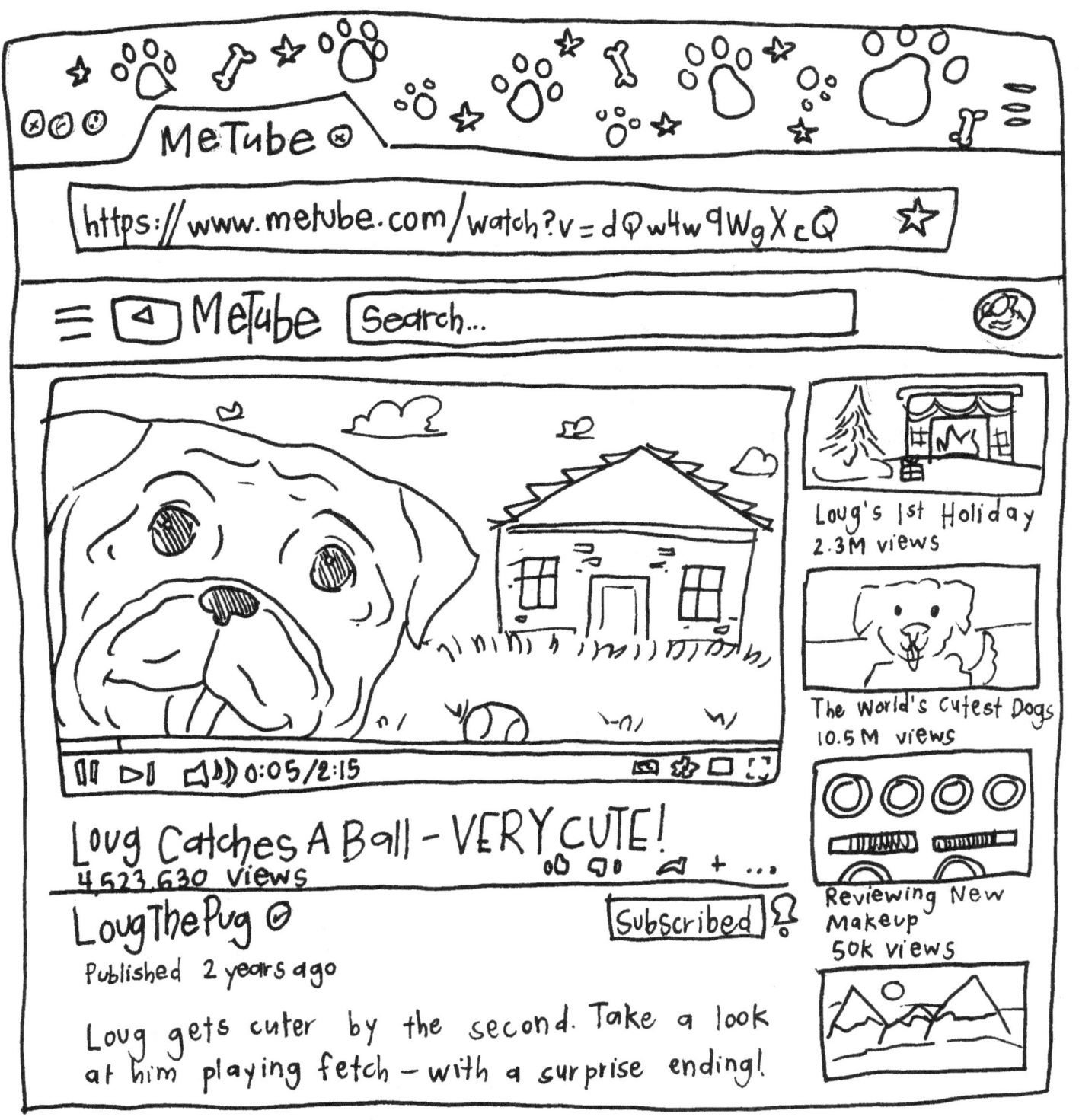

If you're not watching
dog videos, what are you
even doing on here?

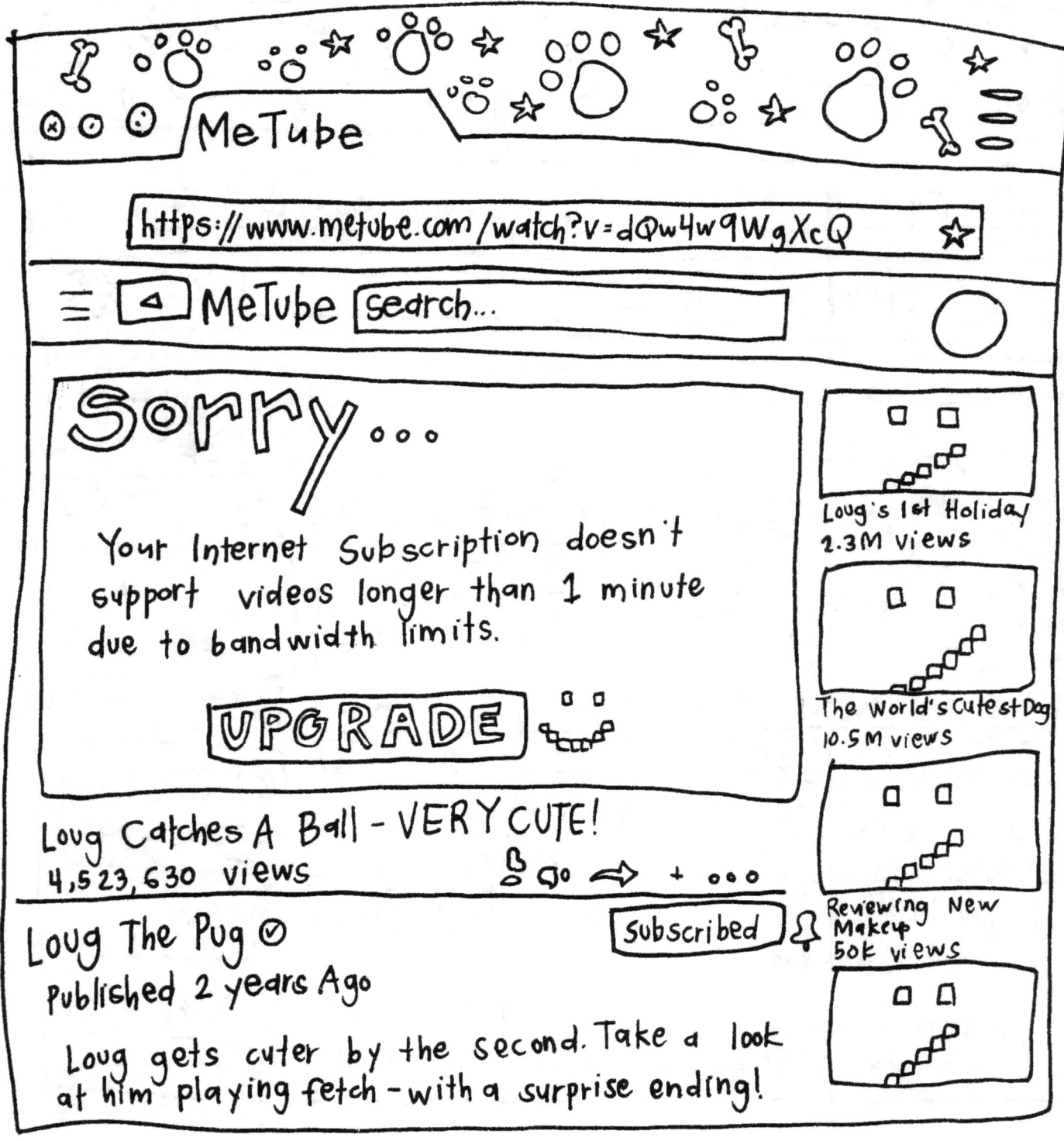

You could just hang out at dog parks until something funny happens...

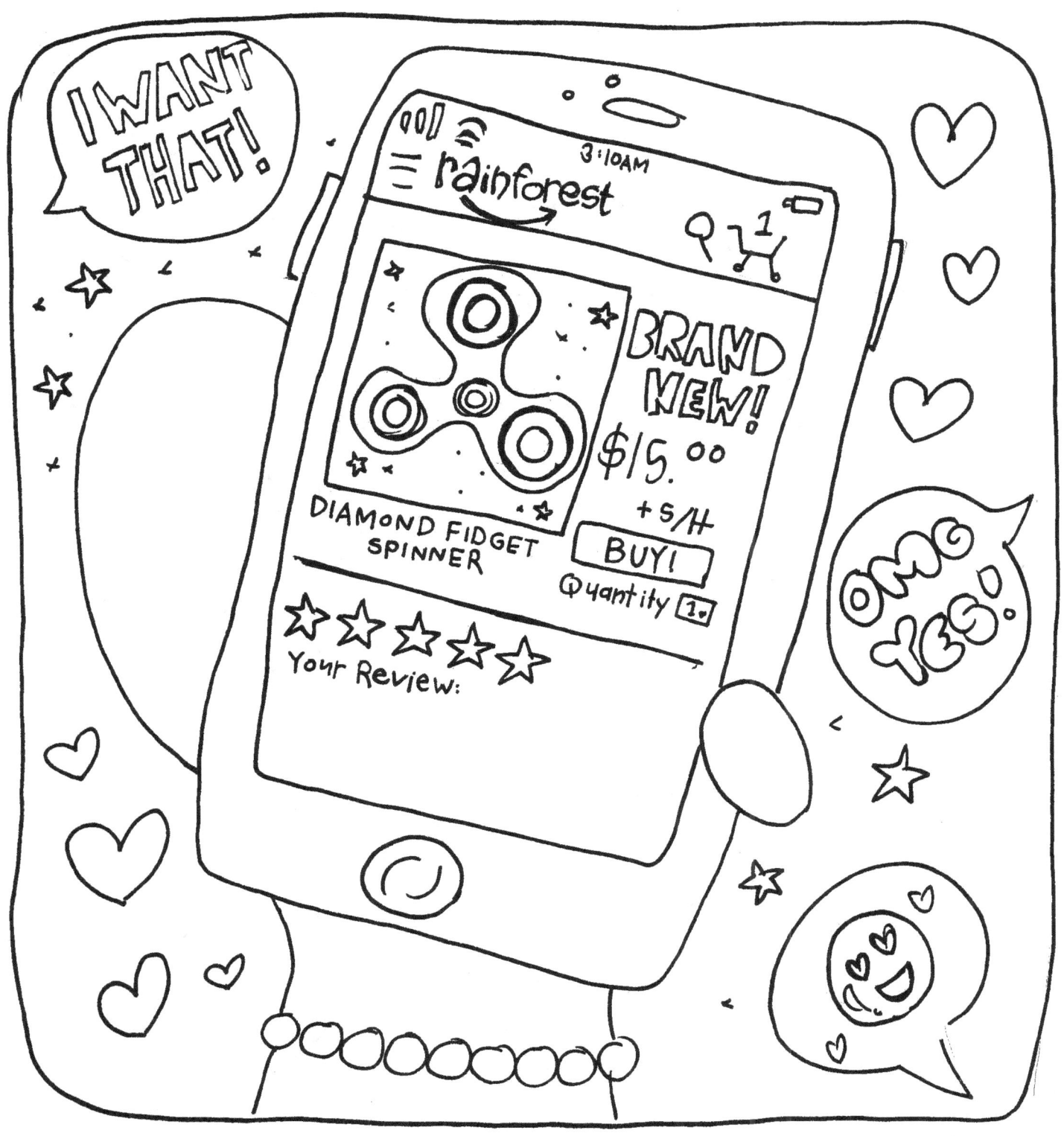

Remember that thing you didn't know you needed? The internet does.

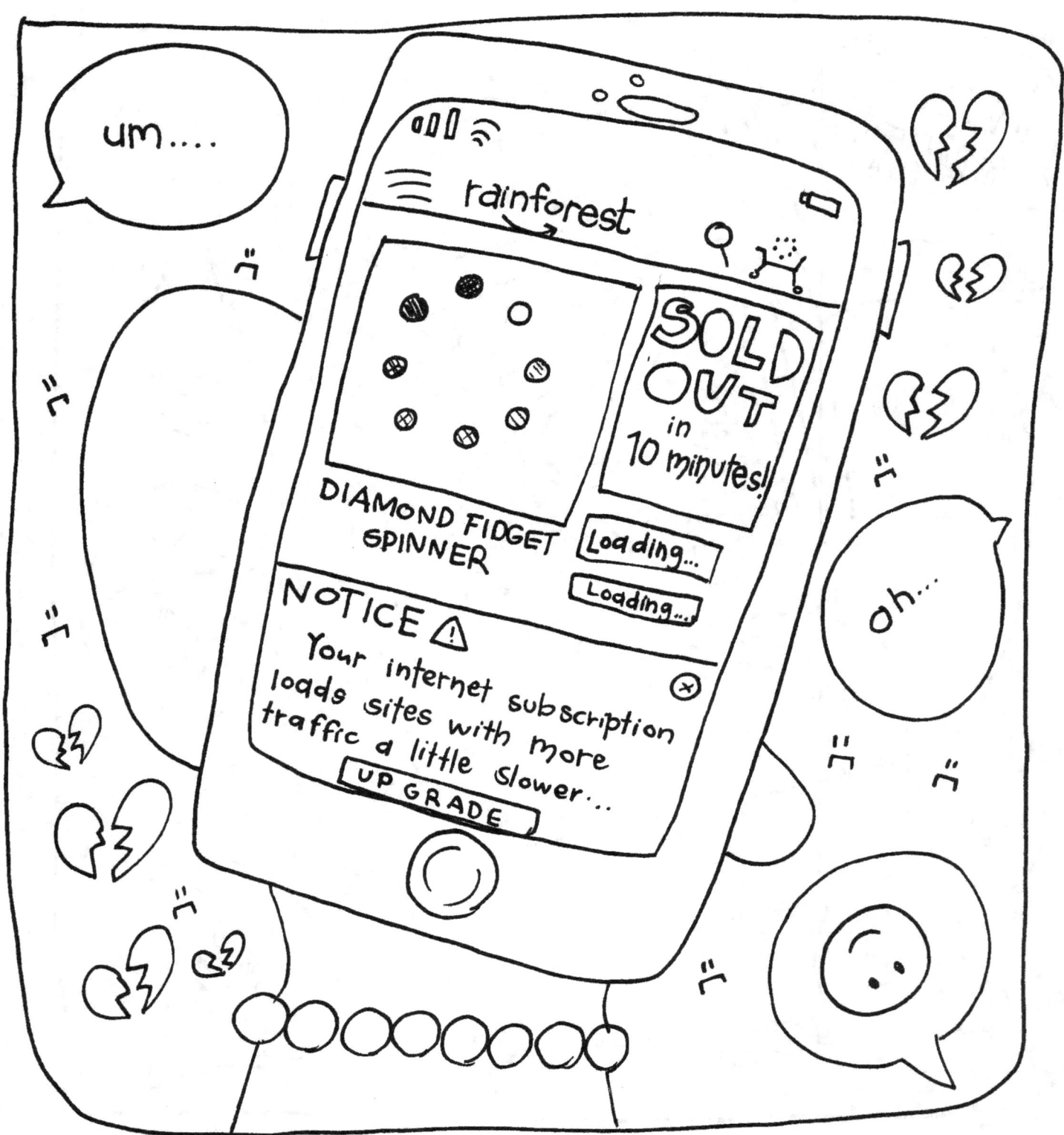

Maybe when the page finally loads it won't be sold out this time.

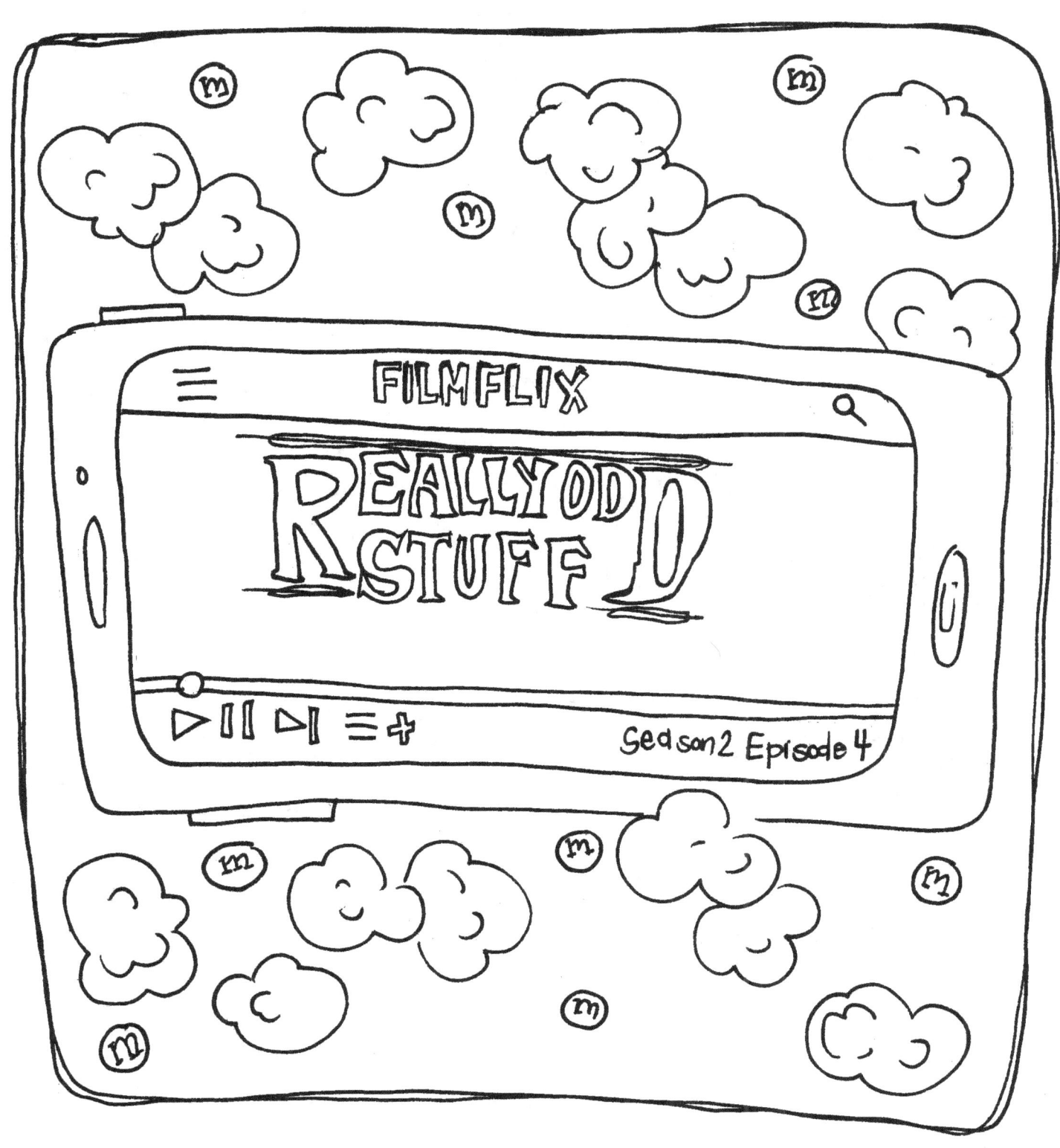

The only healthy binge is one
on the latest show.

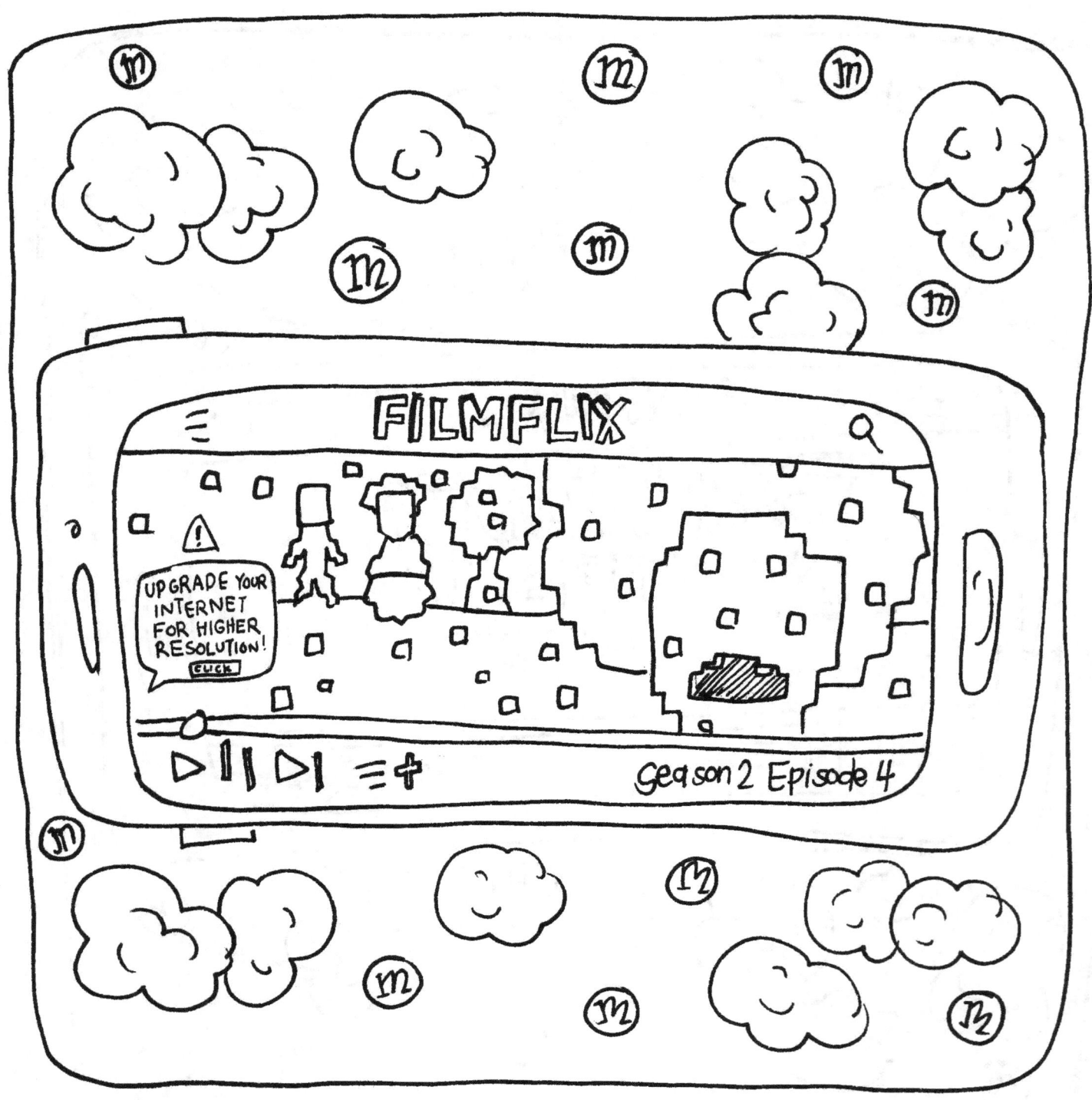

This show is amazing! My
favorite character is the
pixilated - tannish one...no
the other one!

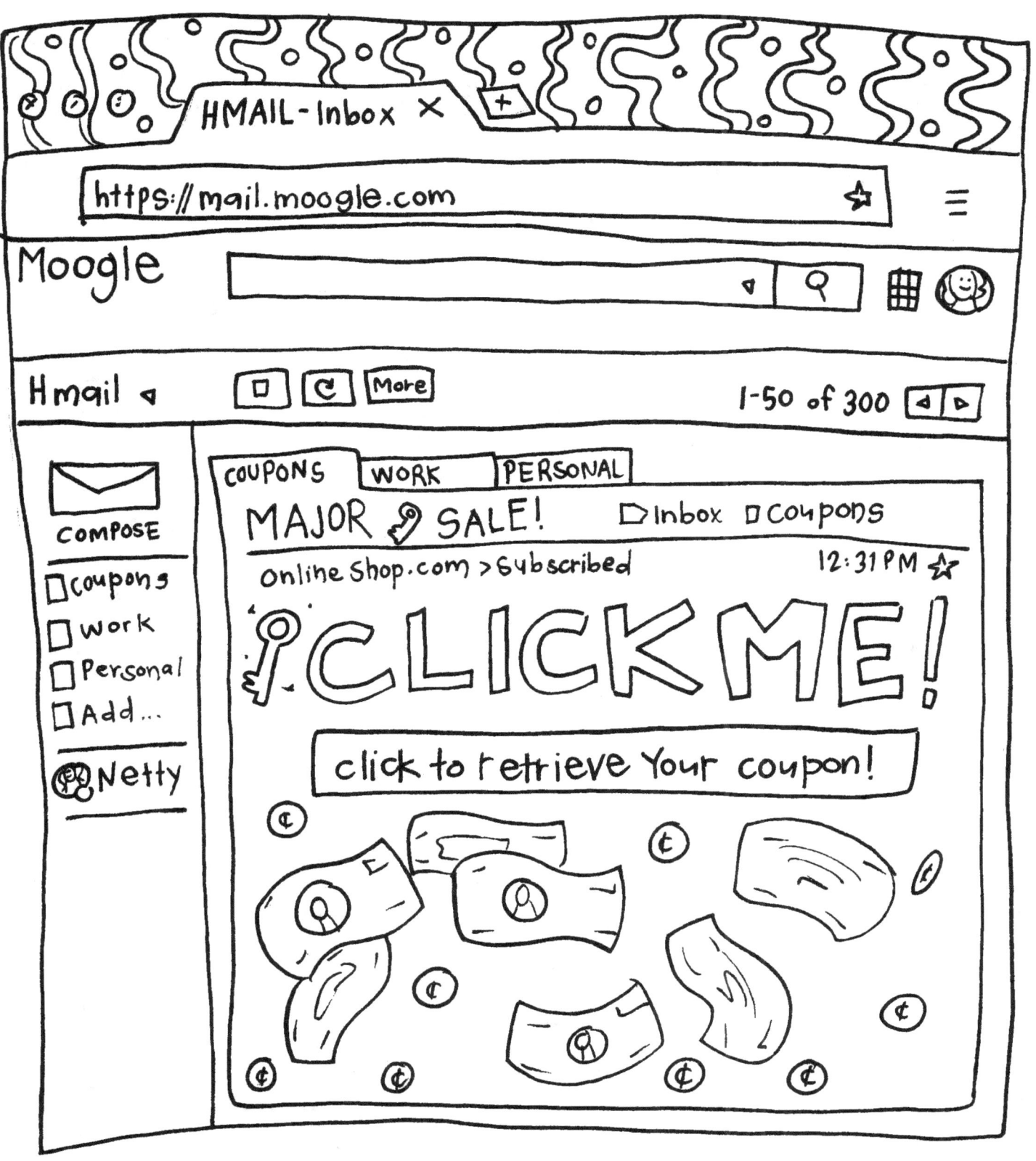

All your life's mail in one spot.

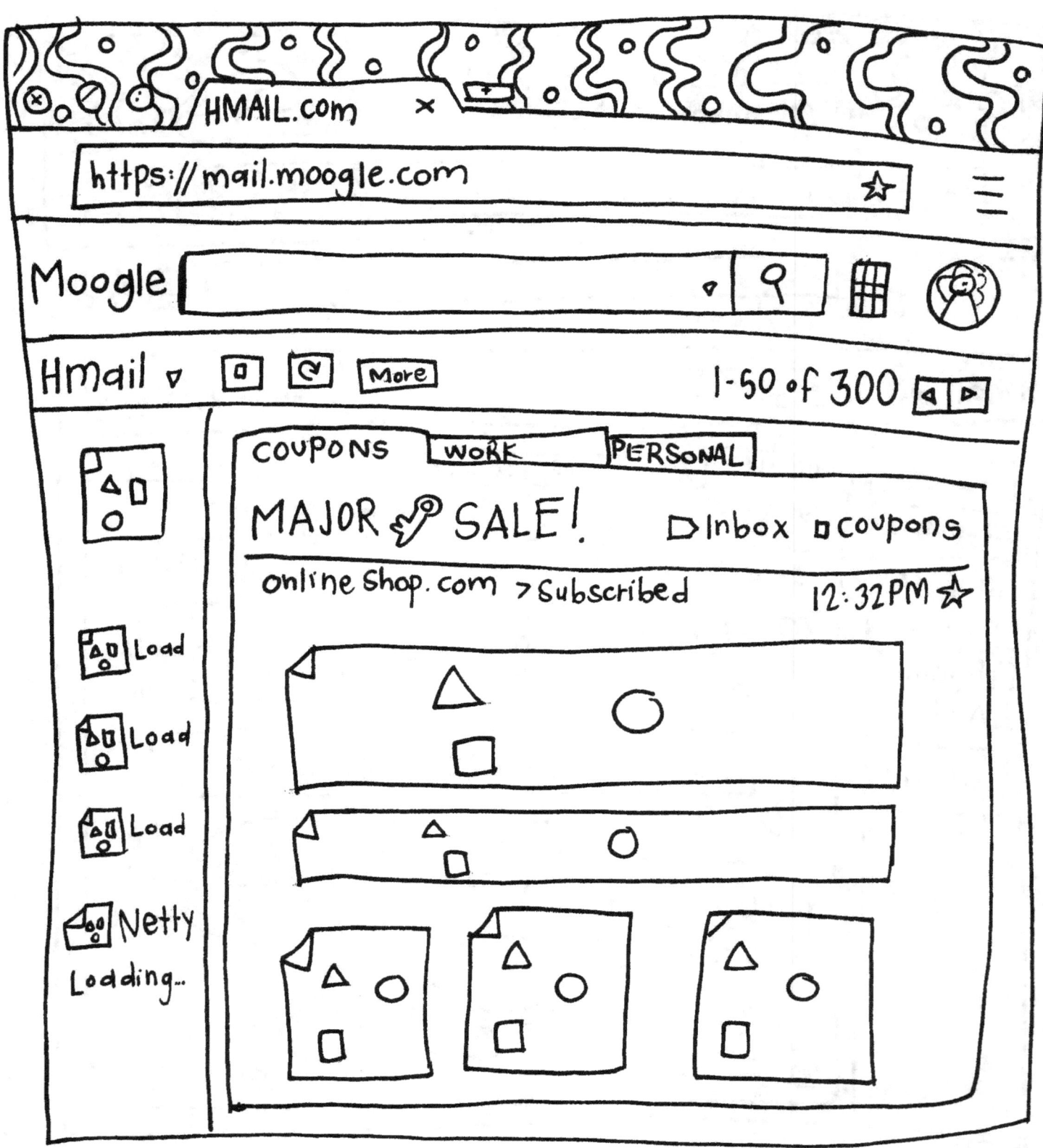

That email with the coupon will
load...*eventually.*

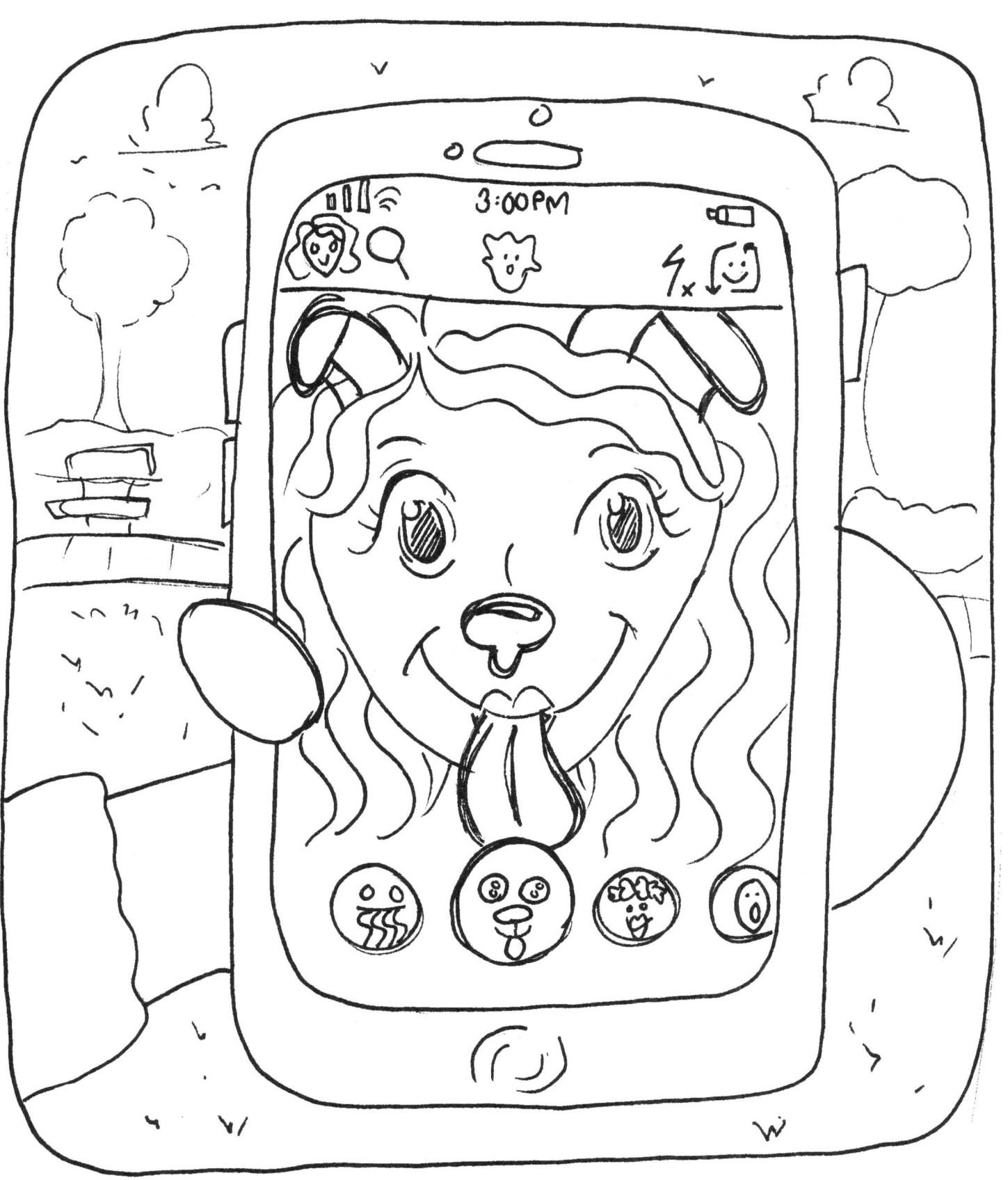

Apply <u>ALL</u> the filters.

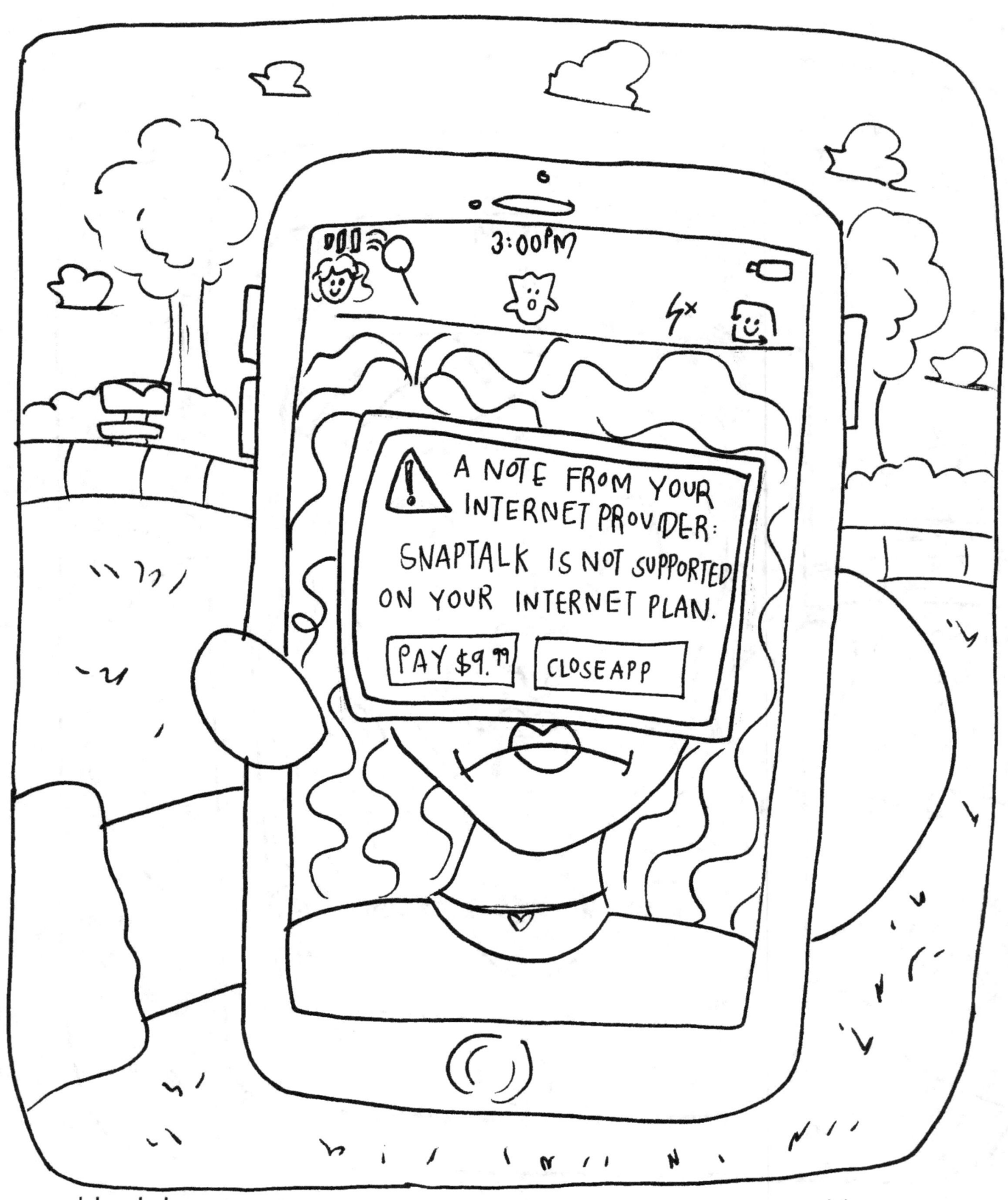

Halloween comes once a year. You
can be a dog then? 20

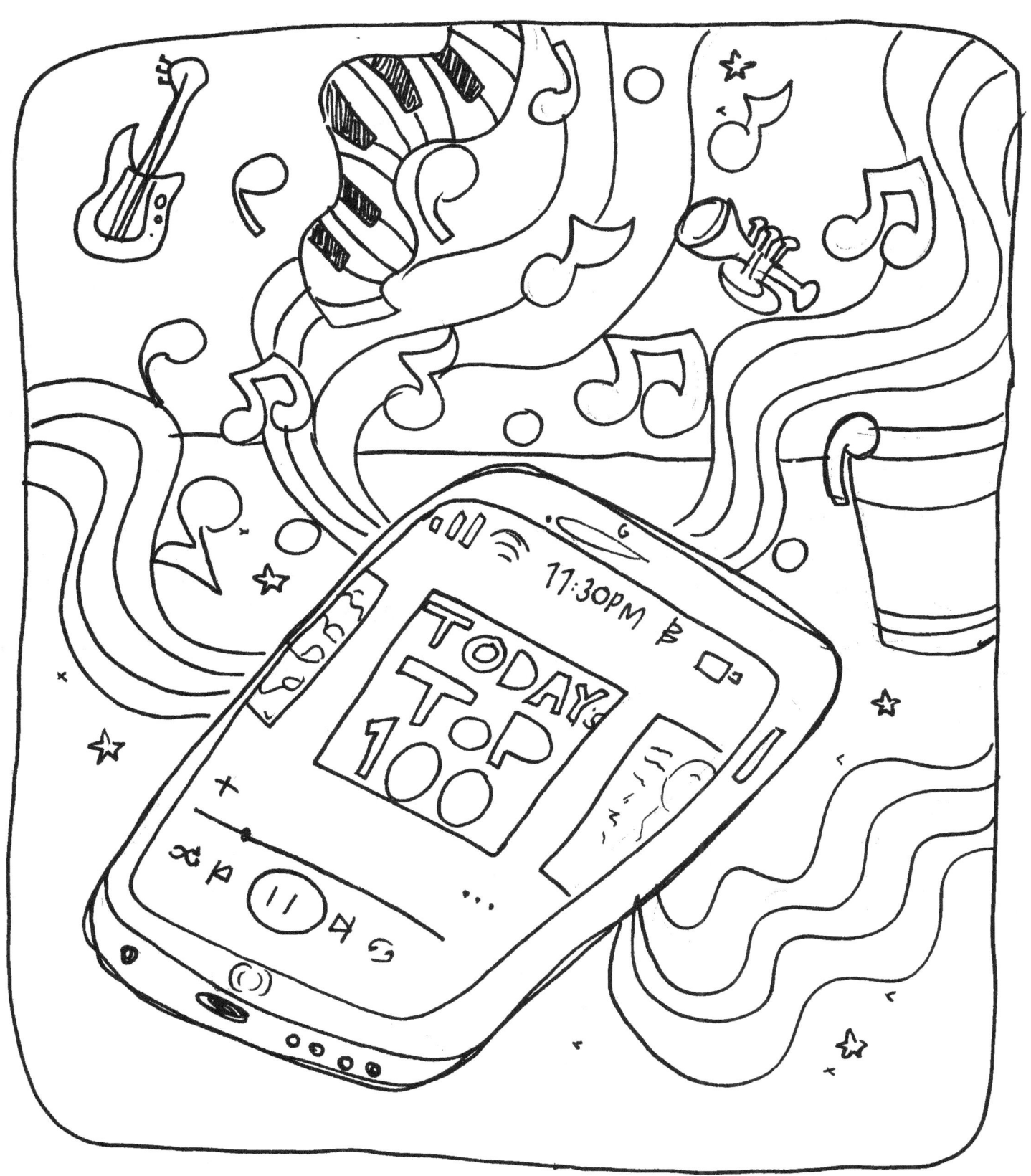

Great to have background
music at parties.

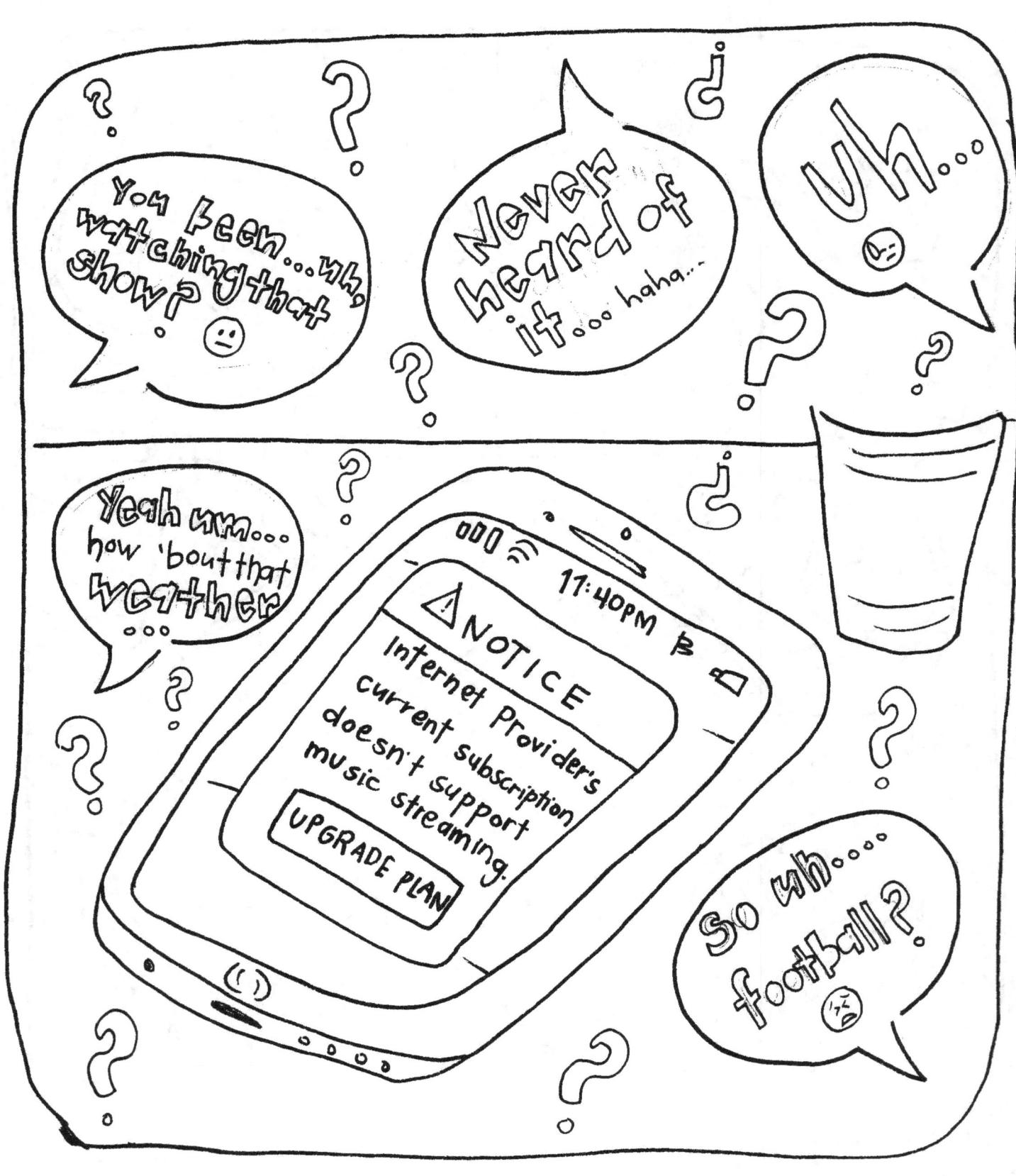

... this is *super* awkward...

Moment of silence.

Enough Is Enough

What can you do to try and repeal this action? You can contact your representatives, submit complaints to the FCC directly, and join action groups to peacefully protest.

There are plenty of resources to help you along the way. Here are a few.

www.savetheinternet.com

www.battleforthenet.com

www.action.aclu.org/secure/FCC-preserve_net_neutrality

With all of our help, we can restore the internet to its rightful uncensored and neutral access form.

Maybe even bring back Vine, too.

ABOUT THE CREW

Timothy Carambat is a web application developer and engineer who probably won't be doing much web application design because of the repeal of Net Neutrality. To show his disgust in this act, he teamed up with a local artist (who conveniently is his girlfriend) to make this simple coloring book.

Find him online before it's too late:
  Timothycarambat. com
  Industrialobject. com

Like the art? Lots more where it came from:
  artbymadicat. com
  @artbymadicat on social media

www.ingramcontent.com/pod-product-compliance
Lightning Source LLC
Chambersburg PA
CBHW081649220526
45468CB00009B/2601